# THE QUEEN

# OF

# BARLOW BEND

## The Story of Claudia Flinn

# JOHN CAULEY

For my grandmother
Virginia Jewett Flinn Cauley
for teaching me
to learn and respect family history
and for my great grandmother
Claudia Beasley Flinn
The Queen of Barlow Bend

Editors
Carmen Kearley
Amy McIntyre
Tom Reid

Library of Congress Control Number:  2018910561

# CONTENTS

# INTRODUCTION

Thirty-nine years ago, my step great grandmother, Claudia Beasley Flinn left this world at the age of 87. She was the only great grandmother I ever had and anyone who ever knew her knew she was quite a character. She made us call her Claude instead of anything grandmotherly. I have so many wonderful memories of her.

I can still remember how excited I was to ride in the back seat of the Volkswagen Beetle with Mama and Daddy to Barlow Bend to visit Claude. We'd turn off the road at Gainestown and head down the road until the pavement ended at the dusty red dirt road. To the right was Mr. Eddie Karr's store, where Claude used to work part time, and to the left and down the road was an old wooden house with a screened in dog trot down the center. This is where Claude had lived all alone for many years after my Great Grandfather died in 1938.

Going to visit Claude while she was working at Mr. Karr's store was a treat! I can remember the old red Coke box and getting to reach in and get an ice-cold bottled Coke. I used to love that certain cold, clean smell inside the ice box and then getting to pop the top off the bottle in the built-in bottle opener on the front of the heavy metal box. We would get a loaf of the freshest bread and wrap a slice around a red-hot link sausage, take a seat in the deer skin covered chairs and have our feast! The visit with Mr. Karr and Claude was priceless.

When we would visit at her house, we always had a certain way of letting her know we had arrived. When we got out of the car, we would yell "whoopeeee!" and wait for her to sling open the screen door and yell "whoopeeee!" back to us! We would then enter the little fenced in yard, perfectly scraped clean of every single blade of grass, circle around the rose bed lined with big limestone rocks and get a big hug from Claude.

Claude had electricity, butane gas in a big silver bullet shaped tank beside the old house for heat and cooking, but no running water. And she would not change a thing. I couldn't wait to get in the house to grab her water buckets and walk down the hill in the back to the spring to get water for her. We would bring the buckets in to her kitchen and get the big tin dipper to fill our glasses with the best water ever as our reward. By the time we got back, she had prepared Sanka coffee for Mama and Daddy. Mama used to say it was so strong, her spoon would stand straight up in it by itself. Claude would always have Stage Planks, a big cookie with pink icing, as our treat.

I do believe I could write a book about Claude. I'd title it "The Queen of Barlow Bend." I'd tell about the "toddies" she would make from the alcohol all the hunters would bring her during hunting season. Or the jokes, some quite spicy, she used to tell that she had typed and neatly folded in that purse that never left her arm. Or the time at Sunday Homecoming, when she got up in the middle of the sermon and told the preacher she felt like singing a little song. I'm not sure if it was the Holy Spirit or one of those little toddies, but the preacher allowed her to take the pulpit in her green dress coat with the fur collar and she always made sure to let everyone know it was real mink. She turned to the pianist and said, "Don't worry honey. You don't know this one." Her melody sounded like two cats fighting. Then she walked back to the pew and took her seat next to my family who at this time had almost slid completely from view in their seats. I loved Claude and there will never be another! Thanks for allowing me to ramble my memories.

# PROLOGUE

"Let's get this house all cleaned up and get everything ready!" John shouted to Caro, Gertrude and Jen. "Miss Claudia will be here any time!" The girls scurried around the house cleaning and sweeping and dusting and polishing everything they could. This had been their usual job along with tending to little Pauline, Orie and John Jr., ever since their mother had died after giving birth to little John. Caro was sixteen, Gertrude was twelve and Jen just ten years old when their mother died. They had to grow up fast and learn to help with everything around the house.

The memories of losing their mother on that cold March night were still close. They remember huddling outside the bedroom door and hearing the cries of childbirth. And they also remember the cries of their father when he was told Pauline, the love of his life, had not survived.

But they were excited and a little nervous about meeting this new lady in their dad's life. They could tell he was excited and nervous too. And they could tell that this was extremely important to him. So, it was important to the girls too. Although they missed their mother tremendously, they were old enough to realize that he didn't need to be alone. They knew he needed someone to help him with raising his family. They knew their mother could never be replaced, but it would be a welcome feeling to know he was happy again. And they needed to feel again what it was like to be young girls and teenagers instead of having all the responsibilities of running a house at such an early age. So, they wanted everything to be perfect for him.

The house was nothing fancy. There were four rooms, a front porch, a back porch and a dog trot running down the center of the house that connected the two porches. It was dark wood, inside and out, and had never seen a drop of paint. The inside walls were unfinished, but pictures, mirrors, kerosene lamps and clocks hung on the old rough lumber studs just like it was one of the finest houses you'd ever see. The floors were made of rough, wide wooden boards. On the right side of the house was one big room for the children. Three beds filled the room along with chairs, desks and chifforobes for their clothes and belongings. At the far end of the room was a fireplace. It matched the one on the opposite end of the house. They were made of large white limestone blocks carved from the limestone hills that were down in the woods behind the house. Between the fireplaces on both ends of the house and the old wood burning stove in the kitchen, the house stayed plenty warm during the winters.

On the left side of the house, across the dog trot, was the living room or parlor. To the back of the parlor was the dining room and kitchen. The girls had worked hard to make sure everything was perfect. Even the little wooden outhouse in the back yard was scrubbed sparkling clean and stocked with plenty of newspaper and old Sears catalogs.

Just outside the wooden picket fence that surrounded the immediate yard, and out back of the house was a wooded area with a perfect little trail that led downhill to the spring. The path looked as though it had been traveled many times, and it had. It was cool and shaded, with slippery spots where the children had slid down many times bringing water in big buckets up to the house. Other than an occasional snake darting across the path, it was a quiet walk to the spring with only the sounds of birds in the trees and the chatter of squirrels scampering across the branches above their heads. The children were happy to hear the sound of flowing water, signaling their approach to their destination. Getting there and filling the buckets with water was the easy part. Bringing those heavy buckets back up the hill to the house was the dreaded part of the trip. And of course, there was that occasional tragic accident. Making it all the way back up to the house and then spilling every drop of their hard work.

To the right side of the house was John's garden. There he grew food for the family and made sure no one went hungry. The yard inside the fence was in pristine condition for Miss Claudia's arrival. Every blade of grass was scraped clean and all the weeds pulled from the circular bed of roses in the center of the yard. Pauline's roses. Always a reminder of her. But hopefully Miss Claudia would love roses too.

So, the house was ready. The yard looked beautiful. Now to wait for the arrival of Miss Claudia.

John was a tall, handsome man and just thirty-nine years old when his wife died during childbirth. He was left all alone to tend to six children. He was brokenhearted, sad, depressed and had begun to look much older than his years. "How could something like this happen? Why did Pauline have to leave me alone?" he thought to himself. He loved her so much. He couldn't even bear to think about that cold March night. He knew something was wrong when the doctor came out of the bedroom. The cries of childbirth suddenly were silent. The doctor said that he had done all that he could do. "It was probably a stroke," the doctor said, with a sad look on his face. "I'm sorry John. And I don't think that baby boy will make it either." The doctor placed his hat on his head, grabbed his bag and headed out the door. "Call on me if there's anything I can do for you, John" he said.

John walked slowly into the bedroom where his wife lay lifeless. His sister sat in the corner of the dark, cold room holding a crying baby boy. John fell to his knees beside the bed and wept. He held Pauline's hand and begged God to let this not be happening. "God you can't have her now! I love her, and she needs to be here with me and her family! What will I do? How can I go on?" he yelled as he violently wept. John's sister stood and placed her hand on John's shoulder. John looked up as she handed little John Jr. to him. "This is why you have to keep going, John," she said. "This baby right here needs you. And your other children need you. You've lost your wife, but they've lost their mother. We are going to have to do the best we can and take care of these children. Pauline would have wanted that." John stood and looked at that helpless newborn baby boy. He said "You're right Sis. We are going to have to do the best we can. We've got to make sure this little boy makes it first. Get some more blankets for me to wrap him up in. I'll go get some more wood for the fireplace. We will get through this somehow. I don't know how, but we will."

Folks came from all around to attend Pauline's service. It was held at the beautiful little Methodist Church in Gainestown. The original church was severely damaged by a tornado in 1911. The new church had been rebuilt using much of the salvaged materials from the tornado. The church had a tall steep roof with a steeple that housed the church bell. John remembered getting to pull the heavy ropes that hung down the wall by the front entrance to ring the church bell as a child.

John sat on the front pew along with his children. His sister held John Jr. in her arms. "This can't be happening," John mumbled to himself. "We were supposed to raise our family and grow old together." John held back tears. He wanted to be strong for his children. It was so hard. The minister spoke words of comfort, but John felt as if his soul had been ripped from his body. But he had to get through this. He had to stay strong. This was what Pauline would expect of him.

When the service was done, the chosen pallbearers walked the coffin slowly down the aisle of the church as the family followed. They continued walking around and down the side of the church to the cemetery out back. Pauline would be buried here along with many generations of John's family and next to their son Earl who was only one year old when he died of a fever in 1903. The Flinns, who immigrated from Ireland, were some of the early settlers of this small community along the Alabama River. Pauline would be laid to rest with the rest of John's family.

The cemetery was peaceful and beautiful. Heavily ornate iron fencing surrounded the family plot of the early Flinn ancestors who settled this community many years before. John's family plot was just behind that, shaded by tall cedar trees and huge oaks. If this had to be, this is where he knew Pauline would want to be laid to rest. The children said their goodbyes to their mother one by one as they walked past the coffin and each laid a rose from the garden in front of their home. Pauline loved roses. Her beautiful rose garden out front of the home would always be a pleasant memory of her from now on.

John and Pauline were very well respected in the community. Friends grieved for and with John. And of course, everyone said they would help him with anything they could. But he knew that when it really came down to it, he was on his own again, and felt like the whole world was sitting heavily on his shoulders. He had relatives who helped tend to the children, so he could continue to farm the cotton. He had to continue to work to support his family. But he felt so alone. He knew he could never replace the love he had for Pauline, but he didn't want to be alone. He needed someone to share his life and help him with all he had been dealt.

John's family saw how sad and alone he was after Pauline's death. Everyone knew he had his hands full trying to tend to the family and continue to work. He needed help and companionship. He was too young to live the rest of his life alone. He was introduced to ladies at church gatherings, but none compared to Pauline. She could not be replaced, and he knew that. He did want another special someone in his life, and he sure needed the help to tend to all his family. Even though Caro, Jen and Jack lived with his sister Virginia most of the time now, he still had almost more than he could handle.

A friend told John about a newspaper column he had seen called "The Lonely Hearts Club." He told John he should put an advertisement in it. It just might be the way to meet that special lady!

"It couldn't hurt to try!" John said to himself. So, he did. He wrote to the local newspaper and placed a "personal" which said:

*Widower located in Barlow Bend, Alabama. Looking for companionship.*
*Hard worker. Honest. Lonely. Family man. Looking for a lady to share my*
*life. Please respond to this address.*

*Sincerely,*
*John Barnes Flinn*

John anxiously checked his mail every day. There was an occasional

response but nothing of any interest. Then one day a letter came that

would change John's life. A letter from a Miss Claudia Beasley of Newton,

Alabama.

*Dear Mr. Flinn,*

*I am responding to your advertisement in the newspaper. I am a single*
*young lady, living in Newton.  I am enclosing a picture of myself. Please*
*respond if you are interested in meeting. I could come by train,*
*accompanied by a friend.*

*Sincerely,*
*Miss Claudia Beasley*
*Newton, Alabama*

When John saw the picture enclosed in the letter, he felt something he

hadn't felt since his precious Pauline had left this world. The woman in

the picture was one of the most beautiful women he had ever seen. She

had shoulder length wavy brown hair, a porcelain complexion and eyes

that sparkled.  "I absolutely must meet this divine creature," he thought to himself. "She is beautiful! I've got to start making plans to get her to come to Barlow Bend! Or I'll go to Newton! I'll do whatever it takes to meet her!"  John feverishly began to write back to Miss Claudia.

*Dear Miss Claudia,*

*I very much desire the favor of your company in the near future. The train station is not far from Barlow Bend, in Walker Springs. I could meet you there, of course accompanied by my sister. She has plenty of room for you to stay. Her home is just up the road from my humble abode. Thank you for sending your beautiful photograph. I enclose mine. I hope you will want to visit.*

*Yours truly,*
*John Barnes Flinn*


Again, John checked the mail every day, anxiously awaiting correspondence from his new-found love interest. Days and days passed. It seemed like an eternity before the next letter arrived from Miss Claudia.

Then it finally came.

*Dear Mr. Flinn,*

*I have checked the train schedule. I can take the train from the Dothan station and arrive in Walker Springs, after changing trains in Selma. Let's select a date and I will arrange for me and my traveling companion to visit. I look forward to the pleasure of your company.*

*Until we meet,*

*Miss Claudia Beasley*

After many more letters over the following months, plans were made for the arrival of Miss Claudia.

Finally the day came.

John went to his barber, got a fresh haircut and shave. He pulled his Sunday best suit from the chifforobe in his bedroom. His daughter ironed it with the kerosene iron John had saved for and bought for Pauline just before she died. John headed out the door of the old wooden house and made a stop in the rose garden. He picked a handful of pink and red roses to take to Miss Claudia. He put his hat on his head and closed the gate behind him. John cranked the old car, drove up the road to pick up his sister, and headed to the train station in Walker Springs.

There wasn't much in Walker Springs. It had a grocery store with a post office inside, a few homes, and a church. Just outside the grocery store was a spring where sulfur water bubbled from the ground. It had a strong rotten egg smell that floated through the air. "That water is supposed to be good for what ails you," John thought to himself. "I should have brought my water bucket with me. Maybe next time."

John arrived long before the train. He wanted to be waiting on Miss

25

Claudia. He didn't want her to be waiting on him. He stood on the small platform at the edge of the tracks. Off in the distance, he could hear the train. He was nervous and excited all at the same time. He pulled the photograph out of his coat pocket and stared at the beauty he was about to meet in person.

The train approached the station slowly and finally came to a stop. Smoke boiled from underneath as the brakes made a loud grinding and screeching sound. Porters began unloading luggage. John glanced at the picture again and scanned the passengers exiting the train.

Did she miss the train? Did she change her mind? A million questions ran through his mind.

He was just about to give up when he heard a soft voice behind him. "John? Is that you?" John turned, expecting to see the beautiful lady in the photograph he clutched tightly. Instead, he saw a small framed lady wearing glasses. Her long, dark hair was pulled back away from her face, and braided down to her waist.

"Yes! It's me!" he said while wondering who this was that called him by his name. "It's me, John!" she said. "I'm Miss Claudia Beasley!" John glanced at the photograph and then at Miss Claudia. "They kind of favor a little," he thought. "But this was not the lady in the photograph."

"Well it's a pleasure to meet you, Miss Claudia, but you sure don't look like your photograph!" John said looking confused.

"Let me see that photograph," Miss Claudia said. "Oh, my goodness!" she exclaimed while giving her best performance to act surprised. "Why that's a picture of my sister Georgia! I must have gotten it mixed up with my photograph when I mailed your letter! It was certainly a mistake, of course!"

Miss Claudia had arrived!

Soon to reign as Queen of Barlow Bend!

# CHAPTER ONE
# THE ROAD TO
# BARLOW BEND

It was an inside joke in my family. Just how many of those dome light covers in the Volkswagen could I bust out with my head? I busted them out in Grandma Cauley's blue Chevy too. And even one in my aunt's Buick. Daddy kept the auto parts store in the dome light cover business in my hometown of Jackson, Alabama all because of me.

You see, I was bouncing up and down on the backseat of the car with excitement. Long before we had to wear seatbelts because it was a law, I used to sit on the edge of the backseat and bounce all the way to Barlow Bend! Chattering away, I can remember my Mama turning and telling me to calm down or be quiet. She did it in a kind way. I was an only child until I was eight years old, when my parents adopted my sister. I had never had a spanking in my life. Never. And hardly got scolded either. But, I did get told to sit down and quit bouncing up and down in the back seat of the VW bug. I could only contain myself for a few minutes. Then I would start right back bouncing up and down and chattering until suddenly, pieces of plastic were flying all over the car. Yep, I had busted out yet another dome light cover! That flimsy plastic was no match for the head of an excited young boy on the way to see his favorite great Grandmother!

The twenty-seven mile trip from Jackson to Barlow Bend seemed to take forever when I was young. Part of the road was paved. Daddy would make the left turn onto the dusty red clay dirt road. I can still remember looking out the back window and seeing the two circular trails of red dust behind us. The Volkswagen did not have air conditioning. I can remember Mama making us roll up the windows when we met another car on the road. It kept some of that red dust out of the car, but not all. We might be smothering from lack of air, but that red dust was going to stay outside the car.

Sometimes, if we were lucky, we could avoid the dust if there had been a good rain. We might slip and slide in spots, but we would be dust free. I can remember being in the Volkswagen with all the windows shut while Daddy was driving in a good rain storm. It would get as hot as fire in that car, with only some vents that blew down towards the floorboard. The condensation would build up so thick that Mama would keep a rag in the glove box to wipe off the windshield, so Daddy could see.

The road to Barlow Bend was magical to me. There was a creek where we would sometimes stop so I would get to play in the cool, clear water as it ran underneath the old wooden bridge. All the lush green vegetation

32

on the sides of the road and down the banks to the creek always
appeared a reddish color, covered in a fine dust, unless it had just rained.
The old bridge was so narrow only one car could pass over it at a time.
When two cars would meet just as they were about to cross the bridge,
one driver would wave and motion "you go first" followed by the other
driver waving "no, you go first." Eventually one of the cars would cross so
both cars could move on and folks could get on about their business.

I can remember the smell of the old wooden crisscrossed posts
supporting the bridge as I played in the creek running around them. It was
a creosote smell. A wet creosote smell. It kind of burned my nose, but not
so bad that it would spoil my hidden fortress. It was so cool and shaded
under that bridge. It felt a little bit scary, but safe, all at the same time. I
loved the rumble of the cars as they would occasionally pass over, leaving
a trail of red dust behind them. Bloomp, bloomp. There were always two
bloomps as the cars went over. I wondered where they were going and
hoped their trip was as exciting as mine.

The limestone hills that lined the creek were perfect for climbing after
playing in the water. Once you got past the slippery, green slimy stuff that
grew down next to the water, there was a treasure of fossils hidden in

those big limestone hills. I dug shells and all kinds of things out of that limestone. My favorite was a whole sand dollar. It amazed my young mind to think there was once an ocean in Barlow Bend! Claude jokingly said it was back when she was a little girl. I could picture her splashing around the edge of the ocean in a knee length bloomer style bathing suit on the edge of that big limestone hill.

Once, while visiting Claude at her house, I found a large carved arrowhead along the edge of the freshly scraped red dirt road. She said it was one the Indians shot at her when she was a teenager. I was fascinated at how she could have seen the ocean in Barlow Bend and been shot by an Indian too! What an amazing life she had lived!

After a fun time playing in the creek, we traveled a little further up the road to Claude's house. There was a semicircle driveway that was just off the side of the road in front. A fence wrapped around the little front yard that she kept in immaculate condition. The grass always seemed to be tall and unkept outside the fence. Smut grass. There was always tall smut grass where Daddy parked the Volkswagen. Bahia grass is the real name, and it would cover your legs in tiny black seeds.

The fence around Claude's yard was a low metal fence, almost like chicken wire. The wire fence replaced the old wooden fence, after it rotted away, that originally surrounded the yard. But the gate to the yard was still wooden. Once you opened the gate, you walked in to a perfectly scraped clean yard. The large oval rose bed in the center of the yard was bordered by reddish orange and pale white sandstone rocks, gathered down the hill by the spring out back. The bed was always full of blooming roses, beautiful and fragrant.

The edges of the beds always had some type of seasonal bulb blooming, adding a beautiful yellow, white or pink border to the red roses in the center. The rest of the dirt yard inside the fence was dotted with wisteria, gardenia and an azalea here or there. But the focus of the yard was the center surrounded by a scraped walkway to the front porch. On either side of the front porch was more wisteria. The vine contained beautiful and heavy purple clusters of flowers that seemed to always be in bloom.

It was tradition, when we arrived and got out of the car, that I would get to yell the first "whoopee!" to announce our visit. If Claude was in the back of the house, we might have to give a couple more yells as we all joined in, until we heard an approaching "whoopee!" coming from inside. We then knew she would be greeting us on the wisteria lined porch shortly. When the screen door swung open, she would always say "Christmas gift!" which meant our arrival and visit was as good as any Christmas gift she could have ever gotten! She would walk out onto the front porch, wearing her perfectly ironed dress, usually with a belt, dressed as she did every day and looking like she was always about to go somewhere. There were hugs and kisses all around as we were welcomed into the old wooden house.

Claude's house was old, but in good condition. It hadn't changed much from when she lived there with my great grandfather. There was a wide set of steps leading up to a big porch with two wooden rocking chairs that had been painted white at some point. Now they were a dusty red with deep layers of red dust in every crack and seam. The screen door was orange colored from all the dust off the road that curved by in front of the house. The screened in area had been added later to enclose the dog trot down the center. Claude had turned the dog trot into a sitting area. There was another screen door on the back side that led to a back porch where you could see the old ringer type washing machine sitting by the back door.

After you entered the screened in area, there was a door to the right which led to the guest bedroom. When Claude and my great grandfather were first married, that room was where John's children slept. It had three beds lined along the back wall of the long room. The first bed had a tall headboard with beautiful carvings of wreaths and flowers. Daddy said his Aunt Virginia died in that bed and that he sure would never sleep in it. Claude used to always say she wanted me to spend the night with her sometime. "What if she made me sleep in the death bed?" I thought.

The inside walls of this room had never been finished. You could see the exposed framing of the walls with the exterior boards showing through. Claude had it decorated to the best of her ability. Pictures hung from the studs and lace curtains hung in the windows, even though they looked as if they had seen better days. The floors were made of wide wooden boards that had almost become shiny from wear. At the far end of the room was a fireplace. You could tell the stone around the fireplace had been white at one time, but now was a smoke gray from years of use. There was a beautiful carved wood antique clock that sat on the mantle. Claude kept it wound and right on time. Beside the clock was a porcelain-like photo of my great grandmother, my real great grandmother. I always thought that was odd because it was a picture of the first wife. Maybe she left it there because she knew my great grandfather still loved her also. Maybe it was there from when the children still were at home. Either way, it was part of the guest bedroom décor. There was also a strange lion's head Morris chair, a sort of early recliner, that sat by the fireplace at the end of the room. It had a carved lion's head on the front of each arm rest. The eyes had red glass marbles that matched the blood red velvet fabric that covered the seat and back of the chair.

So, in this room, we have a tall back bed where a relative had died, a porcelain photo of my deceased real great grandmother, and a chair with arms decorated with animal heads with demonic red eyes. Come to think of it, that room kind of scared the hell out of me!

On the left side of the screened in entrance was another matching room where Claude lived. This room was complete with a bed, sofa, chair, odd end tables, bookcases, a television with aluminum foil covered rabbit ears, a big trunk in the corner, and a white with red trim porcelain "slop jar" beside the bed. It had a matching porcelain lid and was what Claude used as her inside bathroom, so she wouldn't have to go to the outhouse located at the edge of the backyard.

Let me focus for a minute on that "slop jar" as Claude called it.

Now if I were to spend the night like she was always trying to get me to do, was I going to have to use that slop jar if I had to go the bathroom? What was my alternative? To go out in the darkness to the old wooden outhouse in the back yard? I was born pee shy! Would I get my own slop jar? Where would my slop jar be located? What if I had to do more than just pee? Does one sit on a slop jar or just hover? All of these questions would be of great consideration if I ever decided to spend the night.  In the death bed. With my slop jar. While demonic red eyes were staring at me.

But back to Claude's room. Claude had everything she needed right there in that room. Between the matching fireplace to the guest bedroom and the butane gas space heater, she was able to keep the room quite cozy in the winter.  She did that instead of trying to heat the whole house. The center of the floor in the sitting area of the room was covered with a beautiful blue and white floral pattern linoleum rug. I can remember when she bought it. There was a big selection of linoleum rugs at Andrews Hardware store in Jackson.  I can remember when Mama and Daddy helped her get it. We rode all the way to Barlow Bend, with the car window down, and the linoleum rug sticking out. Anyway, it probably helped insulate the old house just a little.

The walls in this room were unfinished, just like the room across the hall. But the walls and windows were decorated just like it was the finest house you would ever see. Claude kept her favorite things in that room. A painting of Niagara Falls which someone in her family had painted on her honeymoon hung on the wall above the fireplace. I heard Claude say it was crazy that someone would have time to paint such a piece of art on a honeymoon. Claude said she sure wouldn't have had time to paint on her honeymoon!

There was a piece of furniture she called her "secretary." It had a bookcase filled with books behind a door of curved glass. The fold down desk is where Claude kept her bills and checkbook. I can remember her sitting at the desk and writing a check out for my birthday when we visited. Five dollars! That was some big money! When we got back home, Mama realized she had signed the check Mrs. Claude Five instead of Flinn. The folks at Jackson Bank & Trust cashed it for us anyway. That is a good thing about having a small hometown bank where everybody knows everybody.

In the corner, just opposite Claude's bed, was a big trunk. It was old and worn looking, with a brown leather cover and dark wooden straps around it. I was always fascinated by that trunk and I always wanted to know what secrets were held inside. It wasn't until after Claude died that I found the treasures hidden in it.

The door leading off the back of the bedroom went directly into the dining room. The floor had settled over the years, so it was a downhill walk through the dining room to the kitchen. The old rickety dining table, covered with a vinyl table cloth with a felt fabric back, held the tall crystal cookie jar where her Stage Plank cookies with the bright pink icing were kept. Those cookies were always a treat when we visited Claude. Mama and Daddy got a cup of Sanka coffee that was so dark it would turn your teeth brown as you drank it. Daddy used to say that if he got killed in a car wreck on the way home he would still be awake. I got a cup of milk with a couple of teaspoons of sugar and a splash of Sanka, along with my favorite Stage Plank cookie. Delicious!

The china cabinet at the back of the dining room was beautiful to me. It had an unusual carved design on the lower doors, almost a beautiful Oriental design. It looked like dragons with wings. I used to run my fingers across the deep carvings, following the lines of the weeping willow trees that filled the wooden background. The top had a mirrored back where she kept her prized emerald green depression glasses. I would count each one, trying to figure which were the real glasses and which were reflections in the mirror. Claude may not have had much, but she was very proud of what she had.

Behind the dining room was the kitchen. A gas stove had been added as a modern convenience, but centered directly in the middle of the room, was an old iron wood burning stove. Not only could you warm up a cold room with that fine piece of equipment, there were also places to cook on the top and front edge. I can remember Claude using it to heat up water in a heavy iron kettle, but never saw her cook on it. As a matter of fact, I'm not sure Claude cooked too much of anything anyway.

In the back corner of the room was a table where she kept several tin water buckets. Since she didn't have running water, she would hire young boys in the neighborhood to go down the hill to the spring and bring buckets of water to her. It was exciting to accompany my Daddy down the hill to get water for her when we went for a visit. I was glad to get back and fill a glass with the fresh, cool, crystal clear water we had just brought

42

to Claude's kitchen. She kept tin dippers hanging on the wall above the buckets. When she would reach for one of the dippers we knew a joke would soon follow. "Did I tell y'all the one about the preacher who went to visit one of his church members?" Of course, she had told us, but we acted like it was brand new.

"Well, it was hot summertime and the preacher knocked on the door of the house and the ugliest old woman came to the door. He introduced himself and asked if he could get a little water since he was parched. She said, "Why of course, but all my glasses are dirty, so you just go ahead and drink your water from the dipper. I do it all the time." The preacher thought, "Lord, I don't want to drink anything after this ugly old woman, but I'm parched." So, he decided that when he drank out of the dipper, he would drink where the handle attaches. Surely, she would drink from the side. So just as he started drinking, the ugly old woman looked up at the preacher and said, "Well, I'll be, Reverend! You drink out of the exact same spot as I do! I thought I was the only one who drank by the handle!" Of course, laughter followed. I came to realize that even though some of her jokes were not that funny, the humor in them was watching her enjoyment and laughter as she told them.

# CHAPTER TWO
# THE TRUNK

I always remember hearing Claude jokingly say that she and my great-grandfather had met through The Lonely Hearts Club. As a young child, I wasn't exactly sure what that club was, but it seemed to make everyone laugh when she talked about it. She always joked and said that after sending him a picture of herself when she responded to his ad, she said he wrote back saying "I'm lonely, but not that lonely!" As the real story goes, John received a picture of a beautiful woman after she responded to his ad in a newspaper. After months of communication, they finally met.

Well, John met the woman who he had been communicating with but not the woman in the picture. Claude had sent him a picture of her much more attractive sister.

So that's how it all began, with a personal ad, or pen pal column as it was called in those days, in a newspaper. Apparently, there was something about Claude that made him fall in love with her, even though she wasn't who he expected to meet. Or maybe it was the need of having someone to help him with his young family. Whatever it was at first, it turned into a true love story.

I still love to read the stacks of letters that Claude had stored away in an old trunk. She saved every memory of the years she shared with John.

She even had the letter where John asked her parents for her hand in marriage.

*My Dear Mr. & Mrs. Beasley,*

*I guess you will be somewhat surprised to get a letter from me but however I guess Miss Claude has told you that we have become very fond of each other and are expecting to be married sometime in the near future. And I am writing to you and all for your consent. I truly hope that I will prove to you all that one could expect of me. I am hoping that this will be agreeable with the family. With all my best wishes to each and all of you.*

*I am truly yours,*
*John B. Flinn*

When Claude died, and we had the chore of cleaning out her house and going through her belongings, I can remember helping my parents go through that old trunk. It wasn't until after Claude was gone that I learned all the secrets inside. Every treasured memory and every keepsake she had of John was stored there. Even down to a four-foot-long braided lock of hair! I wondered why in the world she had saved such a thing until I read the letters from John. When John and Claude first met and got married, Claude had long hair. John loved her long hair. There must have been a heated discussion between them when Claude got ready for a fashionable 1920's "bob" haircut. In a letter between John and Claude,

John wrote in giant, bold letters,

*YOU CAN BOB YOUR HAIR IF IT WILL IMPROVE YOUR LOOKS ANY AT ALL
but save the tail. I want to have a new suit of clothes made from it. After I
put some upon my head.*

*With love,*
*J.B. Flinn*


In the many letters Claude had saved and tied neatly with a ribbon,
stored in the old trunk, I found that after Claude and John married,
Claude's family talked her into returning to Newton.  Maybe she had a
change of heart about living in the country. Maybe her family convinced
her to have a change of heart. The trunk contained stacks of letters that
John had written to her. In each letter, he was begging her to hurry back
home. They were all written after they were married.

It turns out Claude's family had convinced her that she had made a
mistake by marrying John. They told her that she needed to come back to
Newton instead, of being in the woods of Barlow Bend. Her family wanted
her to come home and help them after Newton had suffered a
tremendous tornado that year. Now, what a little ninety-eight pound
woman could do to help clean up after a tornado is beyond me, but she
went back and stayed there for several months. John wrote her almost
every day.

*My Dearest Little Claudia,*

*Well here I am all alone. I would give most anything to have you here. We had quite a time getting home today from the fields. We had a hard rain just ahead of us but made it home in time for dinner. Believe me, I was tired and done some sleeping last night! Orie says don't forget him. Jen and Pauline have my cold now. Take care of yourself my little doll baby. God knows I want to see my darling. I can't hardly live. I am counting the days. Well, it is late, and I am going to try and get some sleep. Hug your dear self for your lonely John.*

*Love from your devoted husband,*
*John*

Claude's family seemed to have kept her busy when she went back home. In all the letters, she was always attending an event or visiting family friends. Between all the "social happenings" in Newton and all the cleanup from the tornado, her family kept finding reasons for her to continue to stay there instead of returning to her husband.

But love finally won. Claude did return to spend the next twenty years with John.

# CHAPTER THREE
# SNAKEBITES,
# FIREFLIES & MAGIC

Claude wasn't the most motherly person in the world. She did her best to be a mother to John's children, but it just wasn't her forte. The children had been shuffled around after their mother had died, but Pauline and Orie ended up living with their dad and Claude. Jen and John had moved in with John's sister Virginia, just up the road. Gertrude and Caro had gone to live with their mother's sister. Claude did her best to be a mother to Pauline and Orie. She knew John expected that of her.

One year after Claude and John were married, Claude realized that she was expecting their child. John's excitement was short lived when Claude delivered twins, much too early for the babies to survive. John and Claude buried them in a private ceremony, at the family cemetery, not far from where John had buried Pauline just a few years before. Claude didn't want to name the twins. She felt naming the babies would make the memories much harder. After they were buried, she would never mention them again.

While Claude was still recovering from losing the babies, Pauline and Orie were outside, playing in the yard. It was late in the evening. Pauline had a tall Mason jar with a screw top lid filled with air holes. She and Orie were catching fireflies when suddenly, screams came from the yard as

Pauline ran into the house. She had been bitten by a rattlesnake.

John ran to his sister's house for help. Virginia brought a bottle of antiseptic to pour on the snakebite. Pauline's foot began to swell tremendously, and she began to run a fever. She was getting much worse until Virginia's cook, Chloe, told them of an old home remedy for a rattlesnake bite. John and Claude were willing to try anything.

Chloe when out to the chicken yard, killed a chicken, cleaned and cut it up into pieces. She brought the chicken pieces into the bedroom, where Pauline lay in bed, burning up with fever. Chloe placed the pieces of raw chicken around Pauline's swollen ankle and foot and wrapped everything in some old rags. She said a few mumbled prayers in a language no one understood, then walked outside. Family members peeped through the curtains to see what Chloe would do next. Chloe fell to her knees as it suddenly began to thunder. Rain began to pour down hard. She uttered more prayers, stood and began to walk back to John's sister's house. Bolts of lightning danced through the sky.

By the next morning, Pauline's fever was gone. When the bandage of chicken was removed from her foot, the raw chicken had turned black and green. It seemed to have pulled all the poison out of the wound. The swelling was gone. Before long, Pauline was up and good as new.

From that point on, Chloe was consulted when there was an illness. Not only was she the family cook, but she was now also considered the family nurse. Even if her remedies included raw chicken.

# CHAPTER FOUR
# DON'T LEAVE ME, JOHN

W. A. Reed,                    Mobile

58

John was a hard worker. Even when the children were grown and had started their own families, he continued to garden and farm. Even though there was a new store just up the road where he could buy many of the things he had provided for the family, he continued to do what he had always done to support them. He seemed tired. But then he was always tired from all his hard work.

One cold winter morning, a neighbor knocked at the Flinns' front door. "Some of your cows have gotten out of the fence, John," the neighbor said. "I'll wait here on the front porch until you get ready and I'll go help you herd them up."

"Much obliged," John said. "I'll be right out." John headed out into the cold early morning air. He got all the cows back in and headed back home, but not before he became chilled in the cold morning air. No one seemed to notice how ill he was until he was suddenly bedridden with fever. Claude called the family physician to come. He did all he could.

"It's pneumonia," he said solemnly as he shook his head. This was just before the discovery of antibiotics. "There's not much we can do, Mrs. Flinn. I'm sorry."

Claude never left his bedside. "I feel so bad," John said to her. "It's so hard to breathe." Claude kept pillows under his head, kept him wrapped up in blankets to keep him warm and tried her best to break the fever. But it just didn't help.

John fell into a deep sleep as Claude held his hand on that cold December night. "My darling John," Claude tearfully whispered. "Don't leave me."

John was gone.

# CHAPTER FIVE
# THE LITTLE SNAKE

Claude continued to live in the old house that she and John shared. She talked about him all the time, sometimes in the present tense, as if he were still there with her. A beautiful old black and white portrait of John hung by her bedside. He was a young man. It was taken long before he and Claude met. But it was how she chose to remember him. When she talked about her "John," you could hear a different tone in her voice. Whether it was affection or sadness, it was there. Claude had a way of joking through sadness. It must have been to cover her pain and loneliness, but she would always try to make everyone around her laugh.

Claude had always liked being the center of attention. That trait blossomed after John's death. And she had always liked to take a sip of alcohol every now and then. After John's death, that trait blossomed the most! She was always having a little "toddy." But it was for an ailment of some sort, of course.

Barlow Bend was located in a dry county, meaning alcohol could not be purchased there. So, Claude depended on "deliveries." That area of Clarke County, Alabama was a big hunting area. Folks came from all around to hunt deer and turkey in Barlow Bend. She had befriended many of the gentlemen who came from out of town to hunt. Claude met many of the hunters when she went to work part time at the general store up the road. Mr. Eddie Karr's store was the early morning gathering place for hunters as they headed out for the day.

"Could you pick me up a little bottle of bourbon?" she would ask one of the hunters. "I need it to mix with honey and lemon for when I get a sore throat." She would ask that question of many of the men.

"Of course, Miss Claude!" they would reply.

Soon Claude would have enough she could stockpile through the summer months. Claude could always depend on taking several various bottles of alcohol home with her at the end of the day. If you ever smelled alcohol on her breath, she would blame it on her Geritol or SSS Tonic. "Or my rheumatism was acting up and I had to fix me a little toddy," she would slur.

It was always a little scary when she wanted to tell one of her jokes in mixed company, especially if she had consumed a toddy.

Or several.

"Did I tell y'all the one about the little snake that was learning to hiss?" she asked.

"There was this young snake that was trying to learn how to hiss. His mother told him to stay in the pit and hiss, so he stayed in the pit and hissed and hissed. Finally, his mother got tired of him hissing in the pit, so she told him to go to Mrs. Potts pit and hiss. So, he went to Mrs. Potts pit and hissed and hissed. Finally, Mrs. Potts got tired of him hissing in her pit, so she told him to go to his own pit and hiss. So, he went to his own pit and hissed and hissed. Finally, his mother said, "What are you doing hissing in my pit? I told you to go to Mrs. Potts pit and hiss!" The little snake said that Mrs. Potts sent him home to hiss in his own pit. His mother said, "That makes me so mad! I can remember when Mrs. Potts didn't have a pit to hiss in!"

Whew! She made it through that one, but it was close.

# CHAPTER SIX
## CROSSWORDS &
## CUSSING

Claude worked at Mr. Karr's store when he needed her. Since she

didn't drive, he would go by her house and pick her up. It was out of his

way, but he didn't seem to mind. Mr. Karr was a kind, easy going man. His

personality balanced out Claude's sometimes feisty one.

Claude always had a crossword puzzle in her hand. She loved them. She

would buy crossword puzzle books and work through them all in no time.

She would bring her morning newspaper with her to the store and would

work on the daily puzzle when they were not busy with customers.  One

morning, all the hunters began to gather at the store to head out for a

deer drive. Mr. Karr and Claude were busy selling supplies and food to the

men, so she put her newspaper with her unfinished crossword puzzle

down on the store counter. When things slowed down, she reached for

her newspaper, but it was gone. She searched all over the store, but it

seemed to have disappeared. She walked outside to where the group of

men gathered outside the store and yelled, "Did any of you see my

newspaper?"

The group of men got quiet as a young hunter in the back raised his

hand. "The one laying on the counter in there?" he asked.

"Well, I thought it was an old paper and I took it out back to the outhouse with me."

That poor young man didn't know what a cussing was until Claude got through with him. She loved her crosswords. And I bet that young man never touched another newspaper without asking first.

# CHAPTER SEVEN
# MONSTERS
# IN THE WALLS

I'm sure it was lonely living all alone in the house that Claude and John had shared. It seemed she was always asking someone to come visit. "Johnny, why don't you come spend the night sometimes?" she would ask. I wanted to stay but I'll admit I was a little scared to be that far from Mama and Daddy. But I finally got the nerve up to spend the night. She had been begging me for such a long time. I would always look at Mama and Daddy when she would ask me to spend the night. They would say, "It's up to you, Johnny." I was secretly hoping they would say, "No! You absolutely cannot stay!" But I guess in the end it was actually up to me.

The whole house was a little bit scary to me. Everything was a brown wooden color inside and out. There was no paint on the walls. No paint on the outside. Just an old brown wooden house. The wide floor boards creaked with every step. Half of the house on the right side of the dogtrot that ran down the center was at one time used as the guest bedroom. I really hoped that I wouldn't have to sleep over there all by myself. Claude made sure to let me know that she was going to let me sleep on her side of the house, on the sofa in her combination bedroom, living room and bathroom area. Bathroom meaning slop jar beside the bed.

The old house had no air-conditioning and seemed to be a light dusty red color on the inside from the dirt road that ran in front of the house. When the night came for me to go stay with her, I packed my little overnight bag and quietly got in the backseat of the Volkswagen. I did not even bounce up and down. Mama and Daddy asked, "Are you sure you still want to go?" "Yes ma'am, yes sir," I said. "I'm ready."

When we arrived at Claude's house, she was excited to see us. "Whoopee!" she hollered as she threw back the screen door. "Whoopee!" I yelled back to the best of my ability. When I entered the living area, I saw she had sheets, blankets and pillows out and ready to put on the sofa. I was still not convinced that this would be the greatest night I had ever experienced, but I was willing to try.

I watched out the front door as Mama and Daddy drove away, red dust circling up from the back of the Volkswagen until they were out of sight. "OK, so I'm here now," I thought to myself. "May as well make the best of it." Claude turned on the little black and white TV in the corner of the room. She readjusted the rabbit ear antenna, with aluminum foil wrapped around the top, and finally found something that would come in clearly. "That TV signal must take a while to get deep in the woods of Barlow Bend," I thought.

We watched TV until it got dark. The TV seemed to fill the sometimes uncomfortable silence when we ran out of things to say. Claude wasn't the most grandmotherly person I had ever met, but she tried really hard.

She said, "Let's go back in the kitchen and cook us up some supper." I walked with her, downhill to the kitchen at the back of the house. She said, "How would you like fried spam and grits for supper?" I thought, "Well, I've never had spam and grits for supper so I'm willing to give it a try." Before I knew it, she was making fried spam, a little gravy to go over the grits and some biscuits. We sat in the dining room, just off the kitchen, for our delicious supper. The floor sloped downhill in there also. I held on to the edge of the red and white checkered vinyl covered tablecloth, rubbing the felt back fabric as I ate. Claude set the table with her Golden Wheat dinnerware that she had collected in boxes of Duz detergent. Her silverware was made up of mismatched pieces of family sterling and silver plate. We drank from delicate light green glasses that she called her depression glass. I wasn't sure what she meant by that. They seemed pretty happy to me.

Everything was delicious. I was beginning to like this overnight trip. Soon, Claude made my sofa bed and we were getting ready to tuck in for the night. All of the windows were up and the window screens were covered with red dust from the road out front. An oscillating fan sat on a short table in front of the window. I could hear the squeak of the fan as it rotated in one direction, and the vibration as it rotated back, blowing the warm summer air around the room. As I drifted off to sleep, I was suddenly awakened by an old loud pick-up truck rolling down the old dusty dirt road by the house.

"I guess that's something you're going to hear when you have the windows up," I thought to myself. "I'm used to hearing the hum of the window unit air conditioners at my house." I lay there for a while, thinking that I would never be able to sleep. An occasional car or truck would drive by. Claude would snore and snort. But before I knew it, I drifted into a deep sleep. I was so comfortable, wrapped in the soft sheets and blankets on the sofa.

That is, until I was suddenly awakened by the monsters.

You know, the monsters whose heads stick through the walls of the old board house? They were evil looking. They had horns and beards and there were several of them. They kept poking their heads in and out of the cracks of the boards. I was trying to tell Claude, but I couldn't say anything. They were getting closer and closer. I tried to scream and yell, "Help me, Claude!"

Then I suddenly woke up. I rubbed my eyes and looked at the wall. There were no monster heads. There were no evil looking creatures poking their heads through the boards. Thank goodness, it was all a dream. I hoped I could get back to sleep and make it through this night. "I'll just snuggle back in the covers, maybe cover my head in case of monsters and get back to sleep," I said to myself.

Do I really have to pee suddenly? Claude has no bathrooms. What do I do? Do I actually have to use the slop jar by Claude's bed? Then I remembered Claude placed another slop jar just outside the bedroom for me. So, I had my privacy. I sure did miss the modern conveniences of our powder blue tile bathroom with the matching toilet, sink and tub, at home.

Soon the sun started coming up. I had made it through the night! I could hear Claude in the kitchen. She was boiling water for coffee, her usual Sanka coffee. She drank dark, strong, instant, freeze dried Sanka coffee. She said that I could have a little. Of course, it was mostly Pet brand evaporated milk. She kept cans of Pet milk everywhere. There was

Pet milk in the refrigerator. There was Pet milk in the kitchen cabinet. There were cans of Pet milk on a shelf next to the stove. There were cans of Pet milk everywhere! Claude must've really liked it. I had a cup of Pet milk with a splash of coffee and a lot of sugar. And a Stage Plank cookie with pink icing. It was the best breakfast ever!

Soon, it was time for Mama and Daddy to come pick me up. They made the trip back to Barlow Bend. Mama was glad to see me because it was the first time I had ever spent the night that far away from home.

I had survived my first night at Claude's house! I might go back again sometime!

# CHAPTER EIGHT
# SPOTTY BOY &
# GUESTS

It turns out I was not the first young boy to spend the night at Claude's. She would sometimes rent out the extra bedroom, across the dogtrot, to hunters who came in from out of town. We found this poem, written to Claude, in the old trunk. It came from a young boy who had spent the night there, with his dad. It certainly describes Claude's life perfectly. It even talked about Claude's dog, Spotty Boy. I heard many stories about Spotty Boy, when I was growing up. Claude used to sit him in a chair, put a pair of glasses on him and place a book in front of him. It must have been quite a spectacle to see Spotty Boy read. The young visitor entitled the poem, "Miss Claude."

*Down in Barlow Bend lives a fine little lady,*
*Her friends she can count by the score.*
*Though she lives alone in a spot that is shady,*
*She doesn't wish for anything more.*

*Though I said alone I was really quite wrong,*
*She has a family in an odd sort of way.*
*As she goes about her work she usually sings a song,*
*And if you are there you can hear her say.*

*Spotty Boy, Spotty Boy, what are you up to now,*
*And just what did you do with the paper.*

Come go with me for we must go fetch the cow,
This is not the time for another caper.

Who's she talking to did I hear you asking me?
None other than her brown spotted dog.
Now that little doggie a wonderful pup he is,
He's worth more than a pedigreed hog.

Can perform more stunts than a circus can boast,
He can read the paper and walk on two feet.
For his breakfast he demands his milk and toast
If he doesn't get it he refuses to eat.

Sometimes late in the day they can be seen together,
Walking down the path that leads to the spring.
For regardless of the season or state of the weather,
Drinking water to the house they must bring.

Now Spotty Boy rates first but he isn't all she owns,
Miss Claude raises cattle and chicken too.
When she fries herself a chicken the hogs eat the bones,
Junk such as that for Spotty just wouldn't do.

When last summer I visited down in Barlow Bend,
Miss Claude she asked me to spend the night.

*So I write this little verse for her to send,*

*And I sure hope she thinks it's alright.*


*She is a mighty swell person whom we all admire,*

*As independent as a king on his throne.*

*Does all her chores, even cuts wood for her fire,*

*Miss Claude gets along quite well alone.*


*Her friends are legion and you'll be one too,*

*If this fine little lady you chance to meet.*

*Drop by to see her and she'll sure welcome you,*

*With true hospitality that no one can beat.*


*Miss Claude if this feeble attempt to write verse,*

*Has succeeded in expressing my feeling toward you.*

*I spose there's something that I could do worse,*

*I just like you and want you to know that I do.*


The poem was signed "Dan & His Pa." I'm glad they could stay in that scary room. In the death bed. With demonic red eyes staring at them.

# CHAPTER NINE
# TO LEAVE
# OR
# STAY

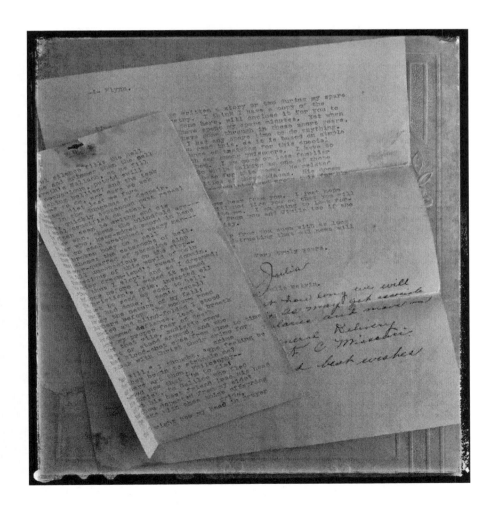

I hardly ever remember Claude having any of her family visit. Her sister, Georgia, came to visit once. She was a very pretty and kind lady. In my young mind, she was a classy, city lady who had made herself come to the country to visit her sister because she felt she had to do it, not because she wanted to do it. I know she wondered why in the world Claude would choose to stay in the woods of Barlow Bend after John died. She was the sister whose photo Claude had "accidentally" enclosed when she answered his "Lonely Hearts Club" advertisement.

Then there was the visit from the twins. Who they were, or how they were related, I have no clue. I remember them always sitting or standing side by side, never smiling. They just looked very serious in their matching plaid dresses with white Peter Pan collars, which they were much too old to be wearing. Their jet-black page boy haircuts didn't have a hair out of place. I don't remember them saying very much. I just remember them looking very uncomfortable in this country setting.

There was a visit from her friend Julia. I'm not sure how Claude and Julia became friends. They were like night and day. Julia was a city socialite. She was on her third marriage, this time to a Harvard graduate who in his spare time, when he wasn't flying to all corners of the world to conduct business dealings, was the World's Fencing Champion, beating a Duke to receive the title. Julia had fallen on hard times after her second marriage but had gotten back on her feet after marrying this husband.

In her spare time, Julia volunteered in the prison system, trying to rehabilitate criminals and find jobs for those who were about to be released. She also wrote very dark poetry, inspired from the men in the prison system. She was a very interesting lady. She constantly tried to get Claude to run away from Barlow Bend with her, to live the city life. If Claude had ever wanted to leave Barlow Bend, Julia was her way out.

But Claude couldn't and wouldn't leave. She wanted to stay in the house that she and John shared. All her memories were there. She felt so close to John when she was there in the house, and Barlow Bend was where she chose to stay.

# CHAPTER TEN
# SHOPPING
# DAY

Since Claude didn't drive, we would ride over and pick her up to come into town. There were just some things you couldn't buy at the general stores of Barlow Bend or Gainestown. Many times, she would just stay a few days with my Grandmother Jen. The back bedroom at Grandma's house was known as "Claude's room." Grandmother loved Claude as her step mother but was slightly embarrassed about the adult jokes she might tell, no matter the company. She also never knew when Claude might fix herself one of those little toddies. So many times, Mama would be the one to take Claude into town to do her shopping.

It was quite an experience taking Claude into downtown Jackson to shop. Mama and Claude had an agreement before they went into one particular store. One of the sales ladies there was known to be just a little bit pushy. When customers would exit the dressing room to see themselves in the full length mirror just outside, the saleslady would always say, "Darling! That just looks wonderful on you! Oh, it's definitely a must for your wardrobe!" It didn't matter what it was. Per their agreement, Mama would stand behind the saleslady and shake her head to signal yes or no, letting Claude know about the clothing. If Mama nodded yes, Claude might strut across the store, looking in every mirror she could find. If Mama nodded no, that dress might start coming off before Mama could shuffle Claude back into the dressing room.

"Claude! Keep your dress on until you get back in there!" Mama urgently whispered as my great grandmother made her way back to the dressing room.

After many wardrobe changes, Claude would leave with several dresses, neatly folded and boxed, handed to me to carry to the car.

"Let's stop by the dime store," Claude requested while walking down the sidewalk towards the car. I remember the smell of popcorn upon entering the bright, shiny red front building which was my favorite place to buy books with my weekly allowance.

"She loves me yeah, yeah, yeah!" we hear coming from across the store, as Claude has put a Beatle wig on her head and started singing and dancing.

"Who is that woman?" one of the employees asked my Mama. "I have no idea," Mama replied.

After a stop by the hair salon at the end of town, where Claude would get a quick cut and set, after announcing "The Queen of Barlow Bend" has arrived, we headed back to the dusty, red dirt roads in Barlow Bend to her little wooden house in the woods.

A big day for Claude, an exhausting day for Mama, and a fun day for me.

# CHAPTER ELEVEN
# I WOULD
# GET THAT
# REMOVED TOO

As long as I can remember, Claude suffered with gall bladder problems. She would get so sick and be bedridden for days. Then it would pass. She would get better and forget that the problem was still there. The doctor had told her that she needed her gall bladder out for years and years. "I'll be ok," she would say. Until another flareup. Then she would be sick all over again.

This time it was different. She couldn't get over this attack and ended up in the hospital in Jackson. This time, it wouldn't pass. The doctor at Jackson Hospital said, "You can't put this off any longer, Mrs. Flinn. You have to let me do surgery!"

At over eighty years old, she lay in the bed and said, "It's going to pass. I'll be ok. Just give me some more of that good pain medicine!"

The pain medicine worked. But it also worked a bit like a truth serum. Not that my great grandmother didn't already say pretty much whatever came to her mind.

"I'm going to send a lady by to visit with you," said the doctor. "She is still here at the hospital, recovering from the gall bladder surgery I performed on her. She can give you some words of encouragement to help you make your decision."

96

A sweet little lady was rolled into the room in her wheelchair. Now I don't want to talk about anyone, but this lady had a mole, a really large mole, smack dab in the middle of her chin. And it was quite hairy.

As we gathered around Claude's bed and listened to this sweet lady share her experience, I could see Claude staring at this lady's chin.

Really staring.

As this lady finished her story, and gave words of encouragement, Claude raised her head from her pillow and from her drug induced state said, "Thank you ma'am! I appreciate all the kind words. If I had a mole that looked like that, I believe I'd let the doctor remove it too!"

An uncomfortable silence filled the room, along with awkward clearing of throats. "And you see that woman sitting over there in the corner?" Claude said as she pointed to a friend. "She thinks she knows everything!"

Her friend smiled uncomfortably and said, "Bless her heart! She's out of her head. She doesn't know a thing she's saying!"

But we all knew the truth serum was working.

"This sure is some good pain medicine!" she said as her head fell back to her pillow.

So, Claude did have the surgery. She recovered and continued to say

whatever came to her mind.

# CHAPTER TWELVE
# HOMECOMING
# &
# DINNER
# ON THE GROUND

Now if you are from the South, you already know what Homecoming Sunday is all about. And if you are unfortunate enough to be from somewhere else, other than the South, I'll explain Homecoming Sunday. It is a yearly church event in the South. Every member, present and past, is invited to attend the special Sunday church service, conducted by a former favorite minister of the church. In the Methodist Church, ministers are rotated to other churches. Claude always said she loved hearing the minister talk about being "called" to another church. She said it must have been coincidence that the "calling" seemed to always include a larger congregation and a larger salary.

But Homecoming Sunday was a big event at the little old white church in Gainestown. During the week before, folks would come from all around to clean up the cemetery just out back of the church. I would ride over to the cemetery with Grandmother Jen, trunk of the car loaded with hoes, rakes and brand-new plastic flower arrangements. Grandmother wanted all the dirt scraped clean around all the graves. It was hard work making the graves look good for Homecoming!

The guest minister would preach up a special sermon, then all the ladies of the church would provide "dinner on the ground." No, food was not actually served on the ground. It was served on tables. Miles of old white painted wooden tables that ran down the side of the church and sat outside in the weather all year, used only for "dinner on the ground" once per year.

As the food was spread out on the table for the crowds to serve themselves, one of the ladies would ask another, "Now which one of those dishes did you cook? I sure want to try some of your recipe!"

Another would whisper, "Now tell me which one of the dishes is the one so and so brought. I absolutely refuse to eat anything that came out of her dirty house! Have y'all seen her kitchen? I just don't know how the whole family stays healthy in that nasty place!"

On this particular Homecoming Sunday, Claude wanted to make sure all of her family was there with her. She had already purchased her new dress on the shopping trip to Jackson with Mama, so she was ready to go. My daddy, his brothers and sister, and my grandmother got up and out early and headed to Barlow Bend to pick up Claude. When they arrived at her house, the first thing they noticed was the smell of alcohol.

"You been drinking, Claude?" Grandmother asked. "Why no, Jen! I just had a little toddy because my throat was a little sore," she replied to my grandmother. "I want to be able to sing well today at church!"

"All the toddies in the world could not help you sing well," Grandmother thought to herself. "I can tell this is going to be an interesting day."

When the family arrived, the church was full. This must have been one of the largest congregations the little church had seen in a while. Folks had come from all around. All the good Methodists had taken the back rows of the sanctuary first, so my family had to sit up on the front row.

The minister said his opening prayer and the congregation had sang a song. Just about the time the sermon had begun, Claude sprung up and headed to the pulpit. Grandma tried to grab her coat tail, but it was too late. Claude walked up to the minister. He backed away from her toddy breath as she said, "Reverend, I feel like singing a little song." I'm not sure if it was the Holy Spirit or that toddy she had earlier, but the minister allowed her to take the pulpit in her green dress coat with the fur collar that she always made sure to let everyone know was real mink. She was barely tall enough to peep over the top of the podium. She looked over at the pianist and said, "Don't worry, honey. You don't know this one." The confused pianist kept her seat as Claude began to belt out a song. Her melody sounded like two cats fighting. When she finished singing to the congregation of wide eyes and open mouths, she headed back to the pew where my family had just about slid completely from view in their seats. The minister awkwardly thanked Claude for sharing her testament and continued with his sermon.

The family never accompanied Claude to another Homecoming, but I bet she went on her own and continued to be the center of attention.

# CHAPTER THIRTEEN
# THE BIRTHDAY GIFT

The ladies in the Barlow Bend community gathered weekly for book reading, cards, sewing, crocheting and tatting. These weekly events were held at various locations as the ladies took turns hosting. After the last gathering, one of the ladies drove Claude back home at the end of the night.

"Do you want me to go inside with you, Claude?" she asked.

"No, I'm fine!" Claude responded.

"What if you go in there, in the dark, and you find a strange man in your house?" she asked.

Claude said, "Why, I would run around the house, lock all the doors and windows and keep him inside!"

When Claude would have the ladies over for the night, she would make sure to be the center of attention as usual. She would have an array of jokes ready to share with the neighbor ladies. "Did I tell y'all the one about the young man who went shopping for a birthday gift for his girlfriend? Let me get my purse because I'm going to have to read this one to y'all!"

Claude dug around in her purse until she found her neatly folded stack of jokes at the bottom, underneath the pack of cigarettes that she thought no one knew she snuck around and smoked. She began to read.

"A young man wanted to purchase a birthday gift for his sweetheart and after much consideration decided on a pair of gloves. Accompanied by his sister, he went to a ready-to-wear store and purchased the gloves while his sister was buying a pair of panties. By mistake, he sent the package containing the panties to his girlfriend as a gift. They were accompanied by this note from him.

My Darling Sweetheart,

This is a token to remind you that I am thinking of you on your birthday. I chose these because I thought you needed them, as I noticed you were not wearing any the last time we went out for the evening. If it had not been for my sister, I would have gotten them shorter, but she said the longer ones were more practical. These are a delicate color. The lady I bought them from showed me a pair she had been wearing for months and they were hardly soiled. I let her try yours on and they sure looked sweet! How I wish I were there to put them on you for the very first time! No doubt many will come in contact with them before I see them. I didn't know the exact size, but I should be capable of judging better than anyone else. Remember when you pull them off to blow in them before putting them away for naturally they will be damp after wearing them. Put them on when cleaning them or otherwise they will shrink. I do hope you will receive and accept them in the spirit in which they were sent. I hope to see you wearing them next Friday night! I am thinking of all the times in the future when I shall be kissing the backs of them!

Love Your Devoted"

One of the ladies immediately volunteered to host the next meeting.

# CHAPTER
# FOURTEEN
# CAT FIGHTS,
# TODDIES
# &
# A SHOTGUN

Claude, a toddy, fighting cats and a gun was not a good combination. "Could y'all ride over and help me with a little something?" Claude phoned to ask Daddy and Mama. "Is everything ok?" Daddy asked. "Yes, I think so. There were a bunch of cats courtin' under my bedroom window last night. I took all the screaming and hissing I could. I went outside with John's shotgun."

"We will be right over, Claude," Daddy said while hanging up the phone. "Lord, what has she done now!"

When we arrived in Barlow Bend a little later, we found Claude had not only shot holes in the side of the old wooden house, she had blasted holes in the old steel drum that collected rain water, for watering and washing clothes, at the corner of the roof line, broke out two window panes in the window of her living area and broke away some of the limestone blocks that supported the old structure. I was glad she missed the old limestone fireplace. For generations, children in the family had carved their names, dates or initials in the soft white stone.

There wasn't a dead cat in sight. She missed every one of them.

After doing a little repair work to the shotgun damaged areas of the house, we patched up the windows until we could get new glass cut to replace the window panes. Daddy told Claude that my great grandfather's gun probably needed some work since the aim was so off. He told her he would take it to get a gun repairman to look at it. He knew it would be best out of her hands, especially when she had consumed a little toddy.

That gun was never mentioned again.

And the cats in the community of Barlow Bend were much safer, as were the neighbors.

# CHAPTER FIFTEEN
# HELP
# ARRIVES

At a certain point, it was obvious Claude needed someone to check on her daily and help around the house. She had no plans to ever leave her house in Barlow Bend. The family told Claude that she would have to hire some occasional help if she planned to stay there. So, she asked a sweet lady who lived just up the road to help her. Her name was Lottie Belle, and she was one of the finest ladies you would ever meet. She was a heavy-set lady, and hugs from her were something I'll always remember. I could feel every drop of love she was giving with those hugs. She did a little cooking and cleaning for Claude. She helped her with her washing and got her sons to go down to the spring to get drinking water. She was a hard worker. She and Claude were found on many occasions taking a little nap when they sat down to watch their "story" as they called it. "The Guiding Light" would be blasting from the little black and white tv, as they both sat in their chairs, heads tilted back, and mouths wide open. You could see the ZZZ's floating through the room and out the screen covered windows.

When Daddy asked Lottie Belle if Claude was paying her enough, she replied, "No sir, she's not paying me very much, but every little bit helps." From that point on, Daddy supplemented her salary so Claude could keep living at home.

Lottie Belle's house was small, and she really needed more room. After Claude died, we moved her and her family into Claude's house. In the lease, Daddy wrote, "Lottie Belle and her family can live in this house as long as Lottie Belle is living, free of charge."

Many times, I would go to visit Lottie Belle in the old house. It was as if family still lived there.

# CHAPTER SIXTEEN
# GOODBYE
# TO THE
# OLD HOMEPLACE

As Claude's health declined, it was obvious she needed nursing care. After only a few weeks in a skilled nursing facility, Claude died peacefully in her sleep just a few days before Christmas 1979, at eighty-seven years old. She was finally with her John again.

The old house that John had built so many years ago to care for his family was struck by lightening and burned to the ground. Lottie Belle and her family escaped unharmed. There was nothing left of the roof, where soothing raindrops lulled me to sleep when I would spend the night, but piles of melted tin.

Many years later, I went back to the old home spot. Trees, shrubs and overgrowth now covered what had once been a beautiful rose garden, cared for, loved and admired by so many. I could barely figure out the path to the spring, but I found it. I found pieces of the door from the front of the iron stove from the kitchen, that kept generations warm, and heated water for a few cups of Sanka.

Claude had a simple life but was such a personable character that I had to share her. You had to know about her even if you never got to meet her.

I had to share her story so that she will never be forgotten.

# THE QUEEN
# OF
# BARLOW BEND

# 1892-1979

# CLAUDE'S JOKES

The Minister

The minister came in the other morning to visit with me a while and sitting there I realized I had no refreshments whatsoever to give him. But I did remember having some sweet milk. So, I asked him would he have a glass of milk and he said yes mam I would enjoy it. So, I went in the dining room to fix it for him and found I had only a half of a glass. But I did have a pint of whiskey on the table, so I just finished filling the glass with the whiskey. And he drank it like he liked it very much. When he had finished he said, "Mrs. Flinn, that's the best milk I ever drank in my life! If that cow of yours ever finds a heifer calf will you please give me first choice in buying it?"

# CLAUDE'S JOKES

Conway Twitty

There was a new minister who moved in to town and he wanted to go around to all his church members homes and introduce himself. He walked up to the first house and knocked on the door. An elderly woman answered and said, "Why you look just like Conway Twitty!" He said "why thank you ma'am but I'm not. I'm your new minister and I just wanted to come by and introduce myself." He went to the next house and knocked on the door. Another elderly woman answered and said, "Why you look just like Conway Twitty!" The minister said, "Why thank you ma'am but I'm just your new minister and I wanted to come by and introduce myself." He continued his journey and knocked on the door of the next house. He could hear a voice say, "Just a minute!" He waited until a beautiful young woman answered the door, wrapped only in a towel, holding it together in the front. As she opened the door, she threw her hands in the air and screamed, "Oh my gosh! It's Conway Twitty!" As her towel fell to the floor, the minister said in his deepest voice, "Hello Darlin'!"

# CLAUDE'S JOKES

I had a visitor the other morning and I decided I would serve coffee. So, I came in with the coffee and I asked the gentleman, "Would you take sugar and cream in your coffee?"

He sternly said, "No thank you. The flavor opposite the milk added to the heat of the coffee causes such a conglomeration until it's almost insuperfractional to my edacadunction."


Church Notice

This afternoon there will be meetings in the north and south ends of the church. Children will be baptized at both ends.

On Wednesday the "Ladies Literary Society" will meet. Mrs. Johnson will sing "Put Me in My Little Bed" accompanied by the Reverend.

On Thursday at 7:00 there will be a meeting of the "Little Mothers Club." All those wishing to be Little Mothers, meet the minister in the study.

This being Easter Sunday, we will ask Mrs. Jennings to come forward and lay an egg on the altar.

# FAMILY GRAVES AT THE
# GAINESTOWN METHODIST CHURCH
# CEMETERY

# FAMILY GRAVES AT THE GAINESTOWN METHODIST CHURCH CEMETERY

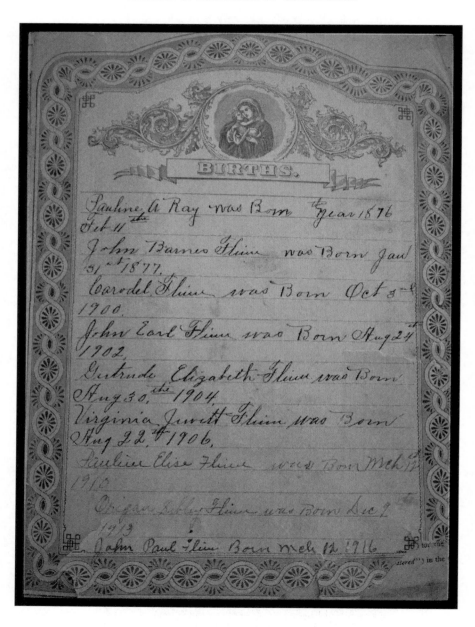

Pauline A Ray was Born the year 1876 Feb 11th

John Barnes Flinn was Born Jan 31st 1877.

Carodel Flinn was Born Oct 8th 1900.

John Earl Flinn was Born Aug 24th 1902.

Gertrude Elizabeth Flinn was Born Aug 30th 1904.

Virginia Jewett Flinn was Born Aug 22 1906,

Pauline Elise Flinn was Born Mch 17 1912

Origen Ashley Flinn was Born Dec 9 1913

John Paul Flinn Born Mch 12 1916

# JOHN BARNES FLINN, RIGHT WITH HIS FATHER ROBERT HEARIN FLINN

# PIECES OF THE IRON STOVE DOOR FROM THE KITCHEN SALVAGED AFTER THE FIRE

Born and raised in Jackson, Alabama,
John Cauley currently lives in Mobile, Alabama.
You can read more writings at
fromthemindofme.com

Made in the USA
Columbia, SC
09 September 2020